POETRY ADVENTURES

BOW-TIE PASTA

ACROSTIC POEMS

BRIAN P. CLEARY

ILLUSTRATIONS BY
ANDY ROWLAND

M MILLBROOK PRESS/MINNEAPOLIS

In memory of
Peggy Murphy Ryan
— B.P.C.

For Lily and Ella
— A.R.

Millbrook Press
A division of Lerner Publishing Group, Inc.
241 First Avenue North
Minneapolis, MN 55401 USA

For reading levels and more information, look up this title at www.lernerbooks.com.

Main body text set in Klepto ITC Std Regular 15/27.
Typeface provided by International Typeface Corp.

Library of Congress Cataloging-in-Publication Data

Cleary, Brian P., 1959–
   [Poems. Selections]
   Bow-tie pasta : acrostic poems / Brian P. Cleary ; illustrations by Andy Rowland.
      pages cm. — (Poetry adventures)
      Audience: Age: 7–11.
   ISBN 978-1-4677-2046-5 (lb : alk. paper) — ISBN 978-1-4677-8107-7 (pb : alk. paper) — ISBN 978-1-4677-8851-9 (eb pdf)
   1. Acrostics—Juvenile poetry. I. Rowland, Andrew, illustrator. II. Title.
PS3553.L39144A6 2016
811'.54—dc23   2014041280

Manufactured in the United States of America
1 – VP – 7/15/15

TABLE OF CONTENTS

What Is an Acrostic?. 4

WHaT Is aN AcRoStiC?

Not all acrostic poems are the same. They can be structured in a variety of ways, but in the ones you'll see here, the first letter of each line forms a word or words when read vertically, or down the page.

The word or message might be a person's name or a subject, with each of the lines helping to define what the poem is focusing on. Like this one:

Bow-tie wearer.

Really likes baseball.

Insanely happy.

Always going places.

Never eats centipedes.

Look down the left side of the page, and you'll see that the poem spells out my first name. The words or phrases built off of that first letter help describe that subject.

Names and other proper nouns are a good place to start, but you can build an acrostic using all kinds of words. Pick a color or a feeling or an action and write it down the left side of the page. Then think of words beginning with each of those letters that relate to your subject. You can also try telling a joke or a quick story in acrostic form. That may take some rewriting. You'll have to be flexible and use synonyms so that your ideas match up to the lead letters of each line. It's kind of like solving a puzzle. Some acrostics rhyme, but most will not, so don't focus on that. Just take out your pencil, write a word vertically down the left side of your page, and start creating a poem of your own.

All kinds of poems are

Cool, but this type is

Really interesting because if you look

Over at the letters going

Straight down

The left side of the page, the first

Initials spell out a word or may even

Contain a message.

Blue gingham

Orange striped

White formal

Tartan plaid

Irish shamrocks

Embroidered stars

Polka dots

Argyle

Silky yellow

Tweed

Awful tasting.

Two hard horns and a third soft one that's

Really a snout made from soft proteins.

Inside its mouth: 200 to 800 teeth.

Can you imagine the dentist appointments?

Extinct, so none are living.

Rumored to be a slow walker.

Ate only plants.

T. rex wanted to have it for lunch.

Older than your parents and even your teacher!

Popular in dinosaur movies.

Seen last alive: 65 million years ago.

Hair-raising hayrides.

Aliens, angels, and awesome parties.

Lanterns being lighted.

Lightning over large Victorian mansion.

October's orange and black holiday.

Witches and warlocks wandering.

Eerie, evil, and exciting.

Eating every bit of everyone's candy.

Nighttime noises.

Parading down Main Street

Is a sea of red-uniformed players of flute

And clarinet and drum,

Navigating their way through confetti and applause.

Only wish that I could march with *my* instrument.

Kissed by the sun, it's

America's wheat grower,

Next door to Missouri. You'll find

Sheep, wheat, cattle,

And acres of corn there.

Summers are hot and tornado-ey.

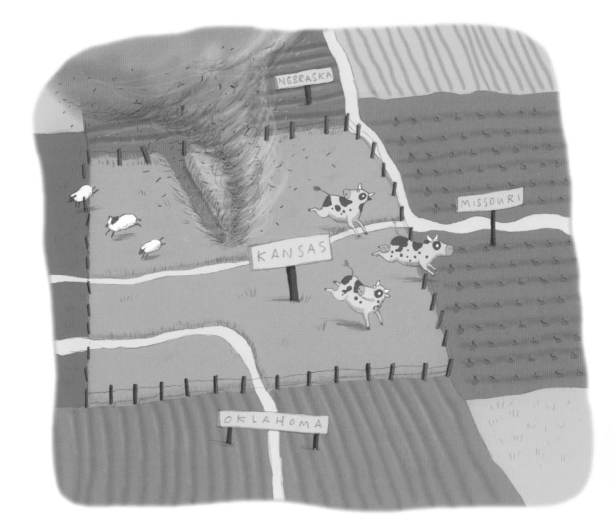

Reading in a cozy nook.

Asking for another book.

I make cookies by the sheet.

Next, they cool. I dunk, then eat.

Yo-yo, board games, watch the rain,

Draw a face inside each pane.

Afterward, I make some s'mores.

Yes, I love the great indoors!

Plums are purple, just like certain grapes, sea

Urchins, and cabbage. The

Rainbow has some purple in its stripes.

Passion fruits are purple, and so are lots of

Lovely birds. Purple sure is pretty,

Except when it's a big bruise on my knee.

Skeletons made of flexible cartilage.

Have multiple rows of teeth.

Active at night, when looking for food.

Really keen sense of smell.

Known to have existed before dinosaurs.

Silly question to ask one: "Wanna go swimming?"

Point: all worn down,
Eraser: black and flat,
Nasty teeth marks,
Chipped, yellow paint,
Inch-and-a-half long.
Lots of good words left in it.

They are the superheroes who show up

Each and every day, not just when some special signal or

Alarm is activated. They answer the call without

Costumes, without masks. Their

Headquarters? A classroom. Their mission?

Engaging and inspiring students.

Rescuing them from boredom, they light the flame of curiosity,

Saving more lives than all those cape-wearing showoffs combined.

Mom, you're there with

Outstretched arms,

To nurture, love, and guide me. To

Help me through

Each thing I do. You're always

Right beside me.

Poop decks, parrots, and planks.

Ill-gotten goods and

Riches that are *tharrrs* for the taking.

Aye! Avast! Ahoy! and *Arrgghh!*

Treasures buried.

Eye-patch-wearing explorers.

Sea dogs, scallywags, and "shiver me timbers!"

Girl walks into a library and gets

In line with the other kids who are

Going up to check out their books.

Girl, when it's her turn, says, "Small cheese pizza, please."

Librarian says sternly, "*This* is a library!" Then the girl,

Ever-so-softly *whispers*, "Sorry . . . small cheese pizza, please."

Peering into my aquarium,

I spy the fish with two

Rows of razor-sharp teeth.

As he swims toward my tapping finger,

Near the top of the tank's glass,

He serves as a reminder that there

Are some pets you should never pet.

First to arrive at emergencies,

It has equipment to

Rescue people and also to

Extinguish fires. It has hoses, axes, and

Turnable ladders. It's usually a

Red and shiny metal

Unit filled with brave people in protective

Coats, pants, helmets, and gloves who

Keep their community safe.

Laser shots toward the net.

Ankle-bending quick turns.

Combines soccer, basketball, football, hockey.

Rock is slang for the ball.

Overhead passes and shots.

Squib-kicking the ball to your teammates.

Scooping and shooting.

Extra-man offense is exciting.

Hidden, nearly, in your jacket of bread, and

Outfitted in crimson and canary yellow,

Tiny beads of water suggest your steamy essence.

Draped in pickled relish,

Onion, chili, or all by your lonesome, in you I've

Got a wiener every time.

Joe, an elephant, and
Olivia, a catfish, got married.
Know what she gave birth to
Eleven months after the wedding?
Swimming trunks.

Suspended in its silky web,

Positioned high in my bedroom's corner,

I want him gone, but not

Dead. Armed with tissue and

Envelope, I nudge him from one to the other,

Relocating him to my sister's room.

Staring out of the

Unopened classroom window,

My eye is drawn to a

Monarch butterfly as it glides to rest on the

Edge of the thermometer that Mrs.

Robbins suction-cupped to the outside glass last fall.

Learn about everything in the universe.

Information in all forms.

Books, books, and more BOOKS!

Real newspapers you can read.

Audiobooks and awesome archives.

Rare maps, prints, and documents.

Your original search engine.

Yolks in eggs and butter and bees,

Envelopes for Easter cards,

Loads of mac and cheese, a lemon twist,

Lights that say proceed with caution,

Omelets, sun, and school buses . . .

Wonder what YOU'D add to this list.

In Southeast Asia, there is a

Nation of many lands:

Desert, mountains, and plains.

Its inhabitants speak hundreds of languages.

And between rainy seasons, it brims with sunlight.

Sunflower seeds or strawberries,

Nachos, nuts, nectarines,

Almonds, animal crackers, apricots,

Cashews or carrots,

Kale or kiwi,

Toast, tangerines, tortillas,

Iced tea,

Mangoes, milk, muffins . . .

EAT!

I am from people who sing away their sorrows, who

Roll their "r's" when they say Mary Catherine Margaret.

I am from strong women and men who can't make a long

Story short. I am from people who can always find

Humor in whatever trouble might be raining down on them.

Poppies are red.

Orchids are blue.

Ever try to rhyme stuff?

Man, it's really hard.

FURTHER READING

BOOKS

Cleary, Brian P. *Rainbow Soup: Adventures in Poetry.* Minneapolis: Carolrhoda Books, 2004.
Discover poems of all kinds in this laugh-out-loud collection.

McNamara, Margaret, and G. Brian Karas. *A Poem in Your Pocket.* New York: Schwartz & Wade, 2015.
During poetry month, Elinor learns about different kinds of poems and is inspired to write her own poetry.

Prelutsky, Jack. *Pizza, Pigs, and Poetry: How to Write a Poem.* New York: Greenwillow, 2008.
Would you like to write your own poetry? Here are some expert tips for turning your own experiences and stories about your family, your pets, and your friends into poems.

Simons, Lisa. *Acrostic Poems.* Mankato, MN: Child's World, 2015.
Learn all about acrostic poems and the different ways they can be written. Discover poems of all kinds in this laugh-out-loud collection.

WEBSITES

Giggle Poetry
http://www.gigglepoetry.com
Find funny poems, poetry contests, and more on this activity-packed website.

Kidzone: Acrostic Poems
http://www.kidzone.ws/poetry/acrostic.htm
Kidzone offers examples of acrostic poems, plus printable worksheets.

Poetry for Kids: How to Write an Acrostic Poem
http://www.poetry4kids.com/blog/lessons/how-to-write-an-acrostic-poem/
The poetry playground of Children's Poet Laureate Kenn Nesbitt has tips about writing acrostic poems as well as other funny poems, games, contests, and lots more.

Young Writers: What Is an Acrostic Poem?
https://www.youngwriters.co.uk/types-acrostic
Find other examples of acrostic poems here, along with an acrostic poem generator to help you practice.